Presented to

Mary

S0-DJM-181

From

Love - Mary Ellen

Date _June 6, 1989_

I Will Lift Up
Mine Eyes

BAKER BOOK HOUSE

Grand Rapids, Michigan 49506

Written and Illustrated by
Samuel J. Butcher

Design coordinator
William Biel

Copyright © 1981
by
Samuel J. Butcher
Company
(All rights reserved)

Published by Baker Book House
with permission of the
copyright owner

ISBN: 0-8010-0962-6

Printed in USA

To
my wife Katie
whose gift is to encourage

When we're uncertain
of the path

and storm clouds gather
in the distant hills,

when barren fields of failure loom

and wisdom seems afar off
when we pray,

when lonely hours threaten us

when trials come
and things we trusted in
begin to fade,

when our heart melts
in the presence of
the unknown,

when friends move on
in search for
something more,

and we are left behind

to think about the moments
that we shared...

even then
we need not be afraid

because our Shepherd's near

we belong to Him;

He knows our need

and binds our
bleeding wounds.

He speaks to us
from Zion's hill

assuring us
we need not fear—
and saying...

"Peace, be still.

I will lift up mine eyes
unto the hills.
From whence cometh my help

Ps 121:1